The First-Time Homebuyers Guide

A Great Resource To Help You Understand The Entire Process

Sherry von Klitzing

Table of Contents

Introduction

Why should you buy a home? We all want a home whether it is a condominium with minimal upkeep but a place to hang our hat after a long day at work or a trip around the world. Women want a home as an anchor. A place of safety, warmth and comfort. Men, take that away and your woman will fly! Not a sexist remark. A psychological statement. Women, ponder this thought.

Home is where the heart is. And yes, you can rent a home but there is always that degree of impermanence. Home is a place where memories are made, children grow up and come back to. These are a few reasons to buy a home. Make your own list right now before we start.

Why I want to buy a home:

What is keeping me from buying a home?

Homeownership has many advantages including:

<u>Equity Build-Up</u>

Making a monthly mortgage payment serves as kind of a savings plan. Over time, you build "equity" in your property that can be borrowed against with a HELOC (Home Equity Line of Credit) or converted into cash when you sell (profit for sale). Tenants paying rent <u>*never*</u> have the opportunity to build equity.

Sound Investment

Over time, your house can significantly increase in value, making it one of your best investments. It can also make it possible for you to move up to a larger home.

Tax Advantage

You will hear people touting about homeownership as a tax advantage. As a tax preparer and financial advisor, I want you to know that unless you itemize your deductions, this is not an advantage. You will need to have a cumulative amount on your Schedule A which is greater than your personal deductions on your 1040 in order to have this as an advantage. For the First-Time Homebuyers I work with, this does not apply.

Security and Satisfaction

Homeownership offers security of knowing you own your home and typically keeps your housing costs stable. Owning a home is the American Dream.

While it may seem that housing costs are simply too high for many people, sometimes it's an even greater risk not to buy. The same house that you can purchase today may cost you much more in the future due to inflation and rising interest rates. In addition, in order to retire, you'll need to build up enough savings and investment to generate yearly income of 70% of your pre-retirement income – a tall order without the capital you can acquire through home ownership.

If you've been thinking of purchasing a home within the next three to six months, you may have some concerns about your ability to buy. You're not alone – many people postpone buying a home for various reasons. The most common reasons include lack of a down payment, insufficient income and credit problems.

This handbook will address these issues and help start you on the path to homeownership.

Ways to Accumulate
A Down Payment

Before we buy anything, we need to know how we will pay for it, whether it is a car, clothing, anything! A house is not different. It is just the single most expensive item most of us ever purchase. Just like when you open a credit card, they want to know that you have a record of paying back and on time. Put yourself in the place of the bank/lender. They are lending you thousands if not hundreds of thousands of dollars so they want to make good and sure that you are in a position to repay the loan and that your record shows you have a willingness to pay your creditors.

Take a look at your spending habits- what you owe and if you pay on time. Even if you have a lot of debt, start organizing your bills and making a plan to pay them down or even pay them off.

There is good debt and there is bad debt. Other than a home, perhaps a car payment that fits your budget, the rest of your "high interest" debt is bad debt. Credit will be covered in more detail a bit later.

One of the biggest problems facing potential homebuyers today is coming up with enough money for the down payment and closing costs. The amount of money you have available can greatly limit or increase your purchasing power.

There are options alternatives to actually saving the money yourself. If you qualify, there are loan programs such as FHA, VA and community grants and loans that can help with low and even NO down payment.

This does not mean you do not need to have money in reserve. While qualifying you, the bank wants to know that you have "reserves" to pay not only your mortgage payment, but taxes and insurance as well.

Once you find the home and your offer is accepted, you will need money to submit with your offer, known as "Earnest Money". In a sellers market, you need to put a chunk down to have your offer considered.

Ernest money goes toward your down payment. This gets credited back to you at closing as part of the down payment. Meanwhile it becomes part of your offer and is held by a real estate company or an attorney, in what is called an "Escrow Account". It cannot be used for anything or anyone until you either buy the home or it is paid back to you if you decide not to move forward or cannot move forward within the confines of the agreement.

What does it cost you to get started? You need earnest money to make an offer. Once your offer is accepted you need a credit card to pay for the appraisal and for the home inspection. **These all 3 come out of your pocket within the first ten days of making an offer that is accepted**.

But Reserves and Earnest Money are not the only "cash" you need. At closing, there are costs involved. Depending on your loan and the lender there are costs for title insurance which the lender requires, with an option for an additional policy for the buyer. The attorney needs to get paid. There are taxes that will be paid upfront depending on what time of year you buy. Homeowners Insurance is required. These, to name a few, are some of the expenses you can expect at closing, even if you don't have to make a down payment. These are "closing costs".

How do you come up with the money to close? You have earnest money, you have inspection, you have appraisal... and then you have closing costs. What if you are that financially set? Read on.

Below are some additional resources that are acceptable to most lenders for closing costs:

1. Have your parents or an immediate family member give you money as a gift. Documentation will be required to prove that the money is actually a gift and not a loan. Any taxpayer is permitted to gift up to $16,000 per year (check to make sure the amount is current. It has increased regularly over the years) to another person without having to pay a gift tax. Technically, your mother could gift you $14,000 and your spouse $14,000. Your father could do the same. This would give you $42,000 for a down payment and closing costs. Check with your lender to see what the parameters are for your loan.

2. Borrow against your 401K or insurance policy. You can also cash out your 401K but you will be subject to withdrawal penalties, payment and taxes. You can use your 401(k) to buy a house without penalty, provided you use a 401(k) loan rather than a withdrawal. Unlike a 401(k) withdrawal, a 401(k) loan is not subject to a 10 percent early distribution penalty from the IRS. The money you receive will not be taxed as income.

3. Sell or borrow against an asset. Selling an asset such as a car can help increase the amount of money you have available. Borrow against an asset is also acceptable as long as you qualify with additional debt.

4. Obtain a low point or zero-point personal loan. This will reduce the amount of your closing costs substantially. A credit card offer at a zero or low rate is **not** acceptable.

5. Ask the seller to pay for all or part of your non-recurring closing costs. Your real estate agent can assist you with this when you make an offer on a home.

6. Ask the seller to carry back financing. If the seller does not need all of the equity in their property, they may be willing to carry some of the financing which will reduce the amount of your down payment.

7. Check into the city and/or county down payment assistance programs.

8. Close escrow late in the month to reduce the amount of prepaid interest on the loan.

9. Use the equity in another property if you own another home you are not selling by getting a home equity loan.

What Type of Credit is Needed to Buy a House?

Your Credit Report

Your credit score tells a lender a lot about your financial background. It is a report card about your behavior in the "School of Money." Any boo-boo's will follow you for at least 5 to 7 years.

Lenders draw from the three top reporting agencies and will use the middle score as your "number." It is a three-digit rating of your quality as a borrower. If high enough, you get the loan. Preferred rating is 680 or above, lowest rating (without issues) can be in the low 600's. And there are some lenders out there that will do into the 560's but they usually find a reason to not write the loan.

This takes into account your credit features such as the number of open credit cards and accounts, how close you are to your credit limits, how you repay or have repaid your credit. Especially tell-tale is how many 30,60,90 day late payments you have over the past 24 months. Late payments can kill a loan right up front. They also like to see how you have handled your available credit. Keep your balances below 30% of your available credit to keep your scores up.

Ways to Improve Your Credit Score

Needless to say, you need to pay your obligations on time. Your debt-to-income ratio will also be a key factor in qualifying for a mortgage. The front ratio will be your housing expense ratio compared to your income. The back-end ratio calculated total debt, including housing, credit card bills, student loans, car payments, etc. compared to how much your monthly income is. You can do the math on this yourself and see where you can cut down your debt. Student loans payments are currently calculated at 0.5% of the loan amount for FHA and 1% for conventional.

With your credit card payments, always pay BEFORE the due date (a few days before is fine) and always pay MORE than the minimum payment to best satisfy your creditors. Hopefully you pay your cards off in full every month due to the high interest they carry, but if you can't, then pay some extra beyond the minimum amount due. These tricks help keep you "under the radar" of being "strapped".

Pre-Approve Before You Buy

You should not pay to get pre-approved, nor should there be a fee to apply for the loan. Many lenders will apply "Junk Fees". These can and should be avoided. When you close, the lender may apply a processing and underwriting fee. Also there may be points (which will equate to dollars) to get your rate. These are discussed later. All of these are normal charges that apply to the closing costs.

Many people shop rates. Rates are rates because they are determined by "the powers that be". They are the same everywhere. Deviations come from the rate you qualify for based on your financial picture, and on a particular loan. Rates vary from FHA to conventional loans to buying your rate down, meaning that you pay for that lower rate in points. The difference in 1/8 of a point or a quarter of a point is insignificant in your monthly payment. The monthly payment is what is important to you, the Buyer! Even if you have bad credit and can get the loan, take it! You can remedy your credit and refinance even after a few months if it makes sense.

Before you begin searching for your new home, you need to determine how much you can afford. You may be able to afford more or even less than you think due to what the lender is willing to lend you based on your income and the amount of down payment you have. By getting pre-approved before looking for a home, you'll save time, energy and frustration because pre-approval:

- **Determines How Much Home You Can Afford**: Pre-qualification helps you avoid buying less house then you can afford or being disappointed if you don't qualify for as much as you had hoped.

- **<u>Shows You What Your Down Payment Will Be</u>**: You'll know approximately how much money you'll need for a down payment and closing costs.

- **<u>Lets You Know What Your Monthly Payment Will Be</u>**: You'll have a general idea of what your monthly principal, interest , taxes and insurance (PITI) payment will be.

- **<u>Identifies the Loan Programs You Qualify For</u>**: With the wide variety of loan programs available, it's important to know which types you qualify for and which best suits your needs.

At this point, the lender also can help you determine alternatives and strategies that could help you buy the home of your dreams. These may include:

- Special first-time homebuyer programs

- Low down payment programs

- Home rehabilitation programs

In order to get a "pre-approval" which most RE Agents require nowadays, your lender will need to know the following:

1. Your employment history and income

2. Your monthly debt and obligations. This will come in the form of a credit report which they will request to pull. Note, a pull from a mortgage company will not harm your credit score.

3. The amount and source of cash available for a down payment/closing costs

After a brief phone discussion during which the loan officer will ask you some general questions about your income, debt, assets, this information will help him/her determine the best type of loan for which you qualify. The loan officer will then study your information and if you qualify will issue you a "pre-approval" letter to give to your RE Agent. This letter will make your offer strong when you find the home on which you wish to make an offer.

How to Increase Your Purchasing Power

There are several factors that lenders take into consideration when determining how much they will lend to you for your home purchase. The three most important factors are your income, debts and down payment. Any one of these factors can greatly impact the amount of mortgage you qualify for. Lenders are primarily concerned with the percentage of your gross monthly income that goes to your new monthly housing expense and your new monthly housing expense plus your other monthly debts. As a general rule, no more than 28% of your gross monthly income should be going towards your monthly housing payment and no more than 36% of your income should be going to your housing payment plus other monthly debt. These guidelines vary by the amount of down payment you make and the loan program you choose.

If you have been pre-qualified and are not satisfied for the amount you qualify for, we have listed four of the most common obstacle to qualifying for a home loan below and some possible solutions to each.

1. **Excessive Debt:**
   a. Consolidate your debts by taking out one loan and paying off your bills with your money.
   b. Pay off long term debts by using some of your cash and making a lower down payment
   c. Selling an asset to pay off bills is another option

2. **Limited Income:**

   a. Income from alimony, child support, bonuses, overtime or future raises might be considered in qualifying.

   b. If you have overlooked any income be sure to tell your loan officer

   c. Find a co-mortgager who is willing to go on the loan with you to help you qualify

   d. Make a higher down payment

   e. Consider a financing option that will allow you to stretch your purchasing power, some of these options include FHA loans, adjustable rate mortgages, balloon financing or a graduated payment mortgage

3. **Credit Problems**

   a. Repair your credit file by contacting creditors and requesting that negative information be removed

   b. Pay off outstanding judgment liens and collections

   c. Re-establish good credit

4. **Lack of a Down Payment**

   a. Get a gift from an immediate family member

   b. Ask the seller to carry back financing

   c. Sell or borrow against an asset

   d. Borrow against or cash out your 401(K)

   e. Ask the seller to contribute towards closing costs

   f. Obtain a loan point or zero-point loan

   g. Consider financing options with low down payments

The Loan Approval Process
Your Real Estate Professional

Using a Real Estate Agent

If you are purchasing a home, it costs you absolutely **nothing** to be represented by a professional, licensed agent. An agent will work on your behalf to

- identify properties to suit your specifications

- schedule appointments to gain access to show

- advise you on price

- Negotiate the deal for you

- Monitor activities for you such as

  o Home Inspection

  o Needs your lender may have

  o Review the Closing Disclosure with you

  o Advise you of contacts for utility services

On behalf of the agent, loyalty is king. A great deal of work is done on your behalf by the agent and money is spent before the agent every gets paid.

Even if you go to a new community, make sure to take the agent with you.

The person working for the builder represents the builder. Your agent will be your very own advocate and can negotiate upgrades, accompany you on walk-throughs (very important) and be of other benefit on things you may not have thought of.

You've taken the first step towards home ownership by selecting a professional real estate agent. You couldn't have made a better decision than to choose a realtor to guide you through the challenging home buying process. You can be assured that you that you will receive the best service with far less hassle and worry. Your real estate professional:

- Helps you assess your wants and needs to find the perfect match between what you can afford and the home that best suits your needs.

- Keeps your personal style in mind when selecting properties to show you

- Accesses all the properties for sale in your desired area by computer. "For Sale" signs and newspaper ads are not always a true reflection of everything that is on the market. Your real estate agent always knows what is available at any given time.

- Negotiates for you. Once you've found the home you want your Realtor will write up an offer and present it to the seller. This gives you the best opportunity to have your contract accepted.

- Gets the right price. Your Realtor is a specialist in your area and knows the market inside out so you will get the best price possible.

- Allows you to make your own decision. A professional agent works for you and respects your opinion. They will not try to force into a decision you don't feel comfortable with.

- Protects your rights. Real estate laws have become increasingly complicated and your realtor is there to assist you in every way.

- Doesn't charge you anything! Your Realtor's services are absolutely free to you – their commission is paid by the seller.

The next step in the home buying process is to identify the type and size home you want/need and select the area(s) you want to look in.

One thing your Agent will know is the type of market you are in. If there are fewer homes for sale (known as LOW inventory) it is a Seller's Market. This means they can pick and choose from the "highest and best" offer that comes in. there is not a lot to negotiate in a Seller's Market and you want to make your best and highest offer to improve your chances of being chosen.

A Buyer's Market is when there is a glut of homes on the market and not many buyers. This could happen because of higher interest rates for example, or over-building in an area. It is in this type of market that the Buyer can negotiate more.

In all of the cases above you will realize that a good Real Estate Agent is your number one advocate in advice, consultation and getting you the home you want with the best possible circumstances.

What to Watch for When Home Shopping

Finding A Home

It's time to go house hunting! Save the gas money and do some research online first. Read about different neighborhoods, and browse listings. Then get a buyer's agent to set up home tours and guide you through the process.

1. Choose a neighborhood and type of house. I always get my buyers to do this before we go out.

2. I set them up to see what's available online. Trulia and Realtor.com are not always updated. Shop thru your agent's resources.

3. Narrow down your choices and see the houses again.

4. Calculate the homes' market value. Your agent will do this for you. He/she wants to make sure your offer is on-target if you really want that house.

5. Make an offer! Your agent will prepare a legal contract for you.

Looking for a Home

If you are new to an area, a financial advisor would tell you to rent for 6 months to determine a community in which you are most comfortable. Determining factors to consider might be:

- Proximity to employment
- Traffic flow

- Schools
- Type of housing
- Restaurants and shopping in the area
- Gated or not
- Social amenities such as community events, golf and tennis clubs, etc.

Work, Play, Live Communities are very trendy in the Atlanta area. This concept keeps dollars in the municipality/community while improving the quality of life by providing amenities such as bike paths, walking trails, restaurants and entertainment without driving.

Gated communities are a popular concept throughout suburban U.S. These communities provide limited access into the housing space, thus increased safety from burglary, etc.

Gated communities are governed by a set of covenants that dictate what is allowed within the community confines. This could include the percentage of dwellings allowed to be rented, the color of the exterior of the home, the landscaping of the home frontage, fencing, etc.

To enforce the covenants, there is a homeowners' committee which is elected to monitor what goes on in the community. Certain expenses are paid for the maintenance of the community such as landscaping, water irrigation, road repair. These funds are collected by a professional management company (HOA) and paid by the homeowner on a monthly or quarterly basis.

Condominiums

HOA fees are also part of condominium ownership. Condominiums are units – usually multi-family dwellings in the form of high-rises and townhomes- where no land is associated with the dwelling.

New Home Communities

With the real estate market developing again in Atlanta, many new communities are being built. A new home is nice for that reason. It has never been lived in.

Considerations for buying in a new community are

- You may have to wait on completion
- If a lot of building out, resale may be difficult

Most buyers today think that they will be in the home of choice for a lifetime. U.S. statistics indicate that we live in a home on average 9 years. Buying a home requires long-term planning, not just with finances, but with your career and your personal life.

If you don't know where you'll be a year from now, let alone seven years from now, you might want to rethink your plans to buy. A house isn't a bargain if you can't recoup your investment. The more time you can spend in the home — comfortably — the better the deal.

For many first-time home-buyers, that means finding a house that suits their needs and their budget now but also offers room to grow — or the option to rent. Location is another sticking point. Many times, buyers will opt for the better house farther out and realize it's not where they want to be. Are you single? Are schools a factor? Airport proximity? Distance from your job? This is why getting a feel for the community, the neighborhood and all logistics are important factors when choosing a location.

2.   Use your imagination. If it is not perfect, what would it take to meet your desires?

Spend some time figuring out how much home you can afford and browse online listings to familiarize yourself with the market. Most first-time buyers are going to be hard pressed to get everything they want, even now. But if you prioritize your needs and wants and give yourself time to look around, you have a better shot.

3.   Don't make finding an agent an afterthought.

With so much information at your fingertips, it might seem old fashioned to enlist the help of a real estate agent. But, a good buyer's agent brings a lot more to the table than listings; she/he can walk you through everything from the loan preapproval to the home inspection and, most importantly, is obligated to put your interests first.

It is better to have your own advocate from day one. It costs you nothing. Seller's and Buyer's agents split commissions paid by the seller. Don't negotiate on your own. Get a professional to help – for FREE!

4.   Don't forget about all the other costs of owning a home.

Most first-time home buyers find themselves focused so much on the sticker price that they fail to account for the other costs that come with owning a home. Some of these costs aren't optional — closing costs, maintenance and utilities. Others — new furniture and gardening tools, to name a few — can add thousands of dollars to the price tag if you're not careful.

Things to observe when home shopping:

- Age – Floor Plan – Square Footage – Traffic Pattern - Stair Width - Hall Width

- Ceiling Height – General Appearance – Heating System – Air Conditioning – Plumbing – Water Supply

- Waste Disposal – Wiring – Insulation # of Entrances – Basement – Attic

You need to make some notes on these interior features. Record important details and note anything that needs changing, repair or special maintenance. You'll avoid costly repairs by making this extra effort.

- Walls – Woodwork – Wall Covering – Paint – Ceiling – Floor

- Floor Covering – Doors – Windows – Windows Treatment – Lighting – Electrical Outlets

- Appliances – Fixtures – Built-Ins – Storage Ventilation – Closets

In addition, investigate any signs of structural or water damage (such as wall cracks, moisture, etc.) When you've actually purchased a home, you'll be doing a walk-through of the property several days before settlement to determine if all the conditions in your contract have been met. However, the time to inspect and not defects you want corrected by the seller is during the contract negotiations and prior to signing the contract. Any repair or replacement items should be noted in the contract or contingent on a house inspection. Your realtor is an expert in this and can assist you with any questions or concerns you might have.

Why a Home Warranty

For seven out of every ten homes, a system or appliance will fail during the course of one year. This is why a Home Warranty is important to the new homeowner. You have your house financed, paid the down payment on it and maybe even bought new furniture. The last thing you have figured into your budget is having to repair or replace something during that first year or two.

The Home Warranty give you peace of mind so with one you can relax knowing that your home is covered from eligible, unforeseen costly repairs. Buyer coverage begins at the close of sale and continues for one year from that date, and is renewable annually if both parties agree.

A Service Agreement with coverage details will be sent to the mailing address provided for the buyer, or if "Go Green" is selected, information will be sent electronically. Payment is due at close of sale and must be received within ten working days in order for coverage to be in force.

A service request must be received during the Service Agreement period. **Your warranty company will pay or reimburse you for costs that have been authorized for a covered repair. Service performed without prior authorization will not be paid.** You are obligated to pay the service fee or the actual cost to repair and/or replace, whichever is less, for each separate service call. A service call means each visit by a service contractor for a single service (plumbing, electrical, appliances, heating and air conditioning and pools/spas). The service fee is due when the service contractor arrives at the home. You may not place a new request for service when any previous service fee is outstanding.

Each warranty company offers several warranties to choose from so make sure to read what is covered, what the deductibles are and the warranty that is right for you. In new construction, homes come with a warranty. Once again, check to see what is covered. It may not be as good as it seems and can be grounds for negotiation.

Your real estate agent will negotiate a warranty for you to be paid by the Seller. If the Seller is unwilling to incur this expense you have the option of paying for it yourself at closing, or even up to 10 days after.

Why a Home Inspection

Another cost that must be paid up-front is that of a home inspection. The inspection is different from the Appraisal. The Appraisal gives the Lender a market value for the house, that is, it determines the fair price of that come compared to others like or similar to it that have sold recently in the area. If there is anything structurally wrong with the home, this is likely to come up in the appraisal.

The Inspection deals with deficiencies in the home. Is everything working as it should? They look for termite damage, proper functioning of electrical equipment such as HVAC, garage doors, etc. He/she will also check simple things as well such as:

1. Try all lights and switches
2. Turn all faucets on and off
3. Flush the toilets
4. Turn on the furnace and air conditioning
5. Test all stove burners
6. Turn the oven on bake and broil
7. Test the garbage disposal
8. Run the dishwasher
9. Open and close all windows and doors
10. And everything else you might not think of

What to Start Collecting Before Applying for A Loan

Lenders require a lot of documentation so it's a good idea to start collecting some of the things you'll need to bring to your loan application beforehand. To save yourself time and frustration during the loan process, start gathering all the documentation listed below as soon as possible.

1. **For Your Residence History:**

    a. Your previous addresses for the last 2 years and how long you lived in each place

    b. If you currently rent, your landlord's name and addresses for the last 12 months

    c. Many times, addresses show up on your credit report that need to be explained. Maybe you have a son or daughter who rented while in college and you signed. Maybe it was an address when you were in college! Expect these inquiries and cooperate with the loan officer if asked to provide an explanation.

2. **For Your Employment History:**

    a. The names and addresses for all you employers for the last 2 years

    b. The dates you worked at each place of employment

    c. A letter explaining any gap in employment in the last 2 years

    d. Original pay-stubs for the last 60 days

e. Most recent 2 years W-2's

f. Most recent 2 years' complete tax returns including all schedules

g. Year-to-date profit and loss statement and current balance sheet if self-employed

h. Transcript or diploma if you were a student in the last 2 years

i. Award letter and copy of most recent check for retirement, social security or disability income

3. **For All Outstanding Loans and Credit Cards:**

a. Coupon book or most recent statement for every account you have open

4. **For All Savings, Checking or Investment Accounts:**

a. The name and address of each financial institution

b. Your account number

c. The current balance or value

d. 3 months' bank statements on all accounts

e. 3 months' statements for any IRA's, 401(K)'s or profit sharing

The Loan Process

The key to a smooth and worry-free loan process is the initial interview. At this time, all pertinent documentation will be requested so unnecessary problems and delays may be avoided.

Within 24 hours of application, a request for a credit report (if not done during your pre-approval) an appraisal on the property is ordered, verifications of employment and funds to close, and any other necessary supporting documentation.

Remember, you will provide credit card information to pay for the appraisal.

As received. the supporting documentation is checked for any problems that might arise. During this time, you will be contacted for more information, or additional items. Stay in touch with your loan officer. Remember, you are not the only file being worked on. The squeaky wheel gets the oil. And if you do have questions, please contact your loan processor.

Once all the necessary documentation is in, the loan officer reviews current programs to ensure you get the best interest rate and terms available. The loan processor then puts the loan package together and submits it to the underwriter for approval.

Loan approval generally takes anywhere from 24 to 72 hours from the time of submission to the underwriting department. All parties are notified of the approval and of any loan conditions that must be received before the loan can close.

The loan is the beginning of the approval process and can take a while so stay in contact with your L.O. until FINAL approval.

Also, the closing statement is carefully calculated to be in line with what has been previously disclosed to you.

Within 1 to 3 days after the loan approval, the loan documents (including the note and deed of trust) are completed and sent to the title company.

A title check is performed to see if there are any liens on the property and that it is the owner of record who is selling the property. Clean and clear title are imperative for the bank to lend on the property. This also protects you, the buyer.

Once all parties have signed the loan documents, they are returned to the lender who reviews the package. If all the forms have been properly executed, the check is issued to fund the loan.

When the title company receives the funding check from the lender, they make the lenders security for the loan a matter of public record. They do this by recording the note and deed of trust at the county recorder's office. Once the loan is recorded, you officially own the home!

THE 10 DO'S AND DON'TS
DURING THE LOAN PROCESS

1. Don't apply for new credit of any kind.

2. Don't close credit card accounts.

3. Don't max out or overcharge any credit accounts.

4. Don't consolidate debt to one or two cards.

5. Don't change or quit your current job.

6. Don't make large deposits into you checking/savings account.

7. Don't make any large purchases.

8. Don't co-sign for any loans.

9. Do stay current on existing accounts.

10. Do call your Loan Officer with any questions regarding the loan process.

An Overview of Closing Costs

Below is an overview of the types of closing costs you may incur on your loan. Some are one-time fees while others reoccur over the life of the loan. When you apply for your loan, you will receive a Good Faith Estimate of Settlement Charges and a booklet that will explain these costs in detail.

Loan Origination Fee: This fee covers the lender's administrative costs in processing the loan. A one-time fee often expresses as a percentage of the loan. Many lenders do not charge this. If yours does, shop around. I categorize this as the largest "junk fee".

Loan Discount: Often called "points" a loan discount is a one-time charge used to adjust the yields on the loan to what market conditions demand. One point is equal to 1% of the loan amount. In this low interest rate environment, it does not make sense to buy your rate down.

Appraisal Fee: This is a one-time fee that pays for an appraisal – a statement of property value for the lender. The appraisal is made by an independent fee appraiser. You must pay for this and provide your credit card information along with your application once your offer has been accepted.

Credit Report Fee: This one-time fee covers the cost of the credit report which is run by an independent credit reporting agency. All lenders charge this. It is something they have no control over and they pull your credit at least twice.

Title Insurance Fees: There are two title policies – a lender's policy (which protects the lender against loss due to defects on the title) and a buyer's title policy. (which protects you). These are both one-time fees. The buyer's title insurance is optional but highly recommended.

Miscellaneous Title Charges: This title company may charge fees for a title search, title examination, document preparation, notary fees, recording fees and a settlement of closing fee. These are all onetime charges. These are 3rd party fees and are charged back to the borrower.

Document Preparation Fee: There may be a separate, one-time fee that covers preparation of the final legal papers including the notes and deed of trust.

Prepaid Interest: Depending on the time of month your loan closes, this charge may vary from a full month's interest to just a few days. If your loan closes at the beginning of the month you will probably have to pay the maximum amount. If your loan closes at the end of the month, you will only have to pay a few days' interest.

PM Premium: Depending on the amount of your down payment, you may be required to pay an upfront fee for the mortgage insurance (which protects the lender against loss due to foreclosing). You may also be required to put a certain amount for PMI into a special reserve account (an impound account) held by the lender.

Taxes and Hazard Insurance: Depending on the month that you close, you may be required to reimburse the seller for property taxes. You will also need to pay an entire year's hazard insurance premium up front. In addition, you may be required to put a certain amount for taxes and insurance into a special reserve held by the lender. This is called "escrow". By escrowing, the lender will pay these costs for you when they come due.

What the Attorney Does

Generally, the Real Estate Attorney provides the following services:

- Requests a title report and policy

- Drafts a deed of trust and/or other necessary documents

- Pays off existing loans when necessary

- Checks for liens on the property and makes sure utility bills are paid to date

- Adjusts taxes and insurance between the buyer and seller

- Computes interest on loans

- Acquires hazard insurance

- Has the buyer and seller sign the documents

- Records the appropriate documents

- Disburses the documents and money to each part involved

Why Title Search and Title Insurance

The title company conducts a title search which is a history of who has owned the property and details all prior transactions, existing items and encumbrances or other factors that affect the title. Your attorney will order a title search and receives a Preliminary Title Report on the property which covered all of these items. This is important to the lender to know that the property is legally transferable to you.

The title company also provides title insurance which protects you and the lender against a '**cloud on title**'. There are two types of title policies:

1. **The Lenders Policy**: Protects the lender against loss due to unknown title defects or other matters that affect title and are not known at the time of sale. This policy is mandatory.

2. **The Buyer's Policy:** Protects the buyer from flaws in the title. This policy is optional but is highly recommended.

When your loan is approved and the loan documents are drawn up, they are sent to the title company or closing attorney, depending on the requirements of your state. Every state is different. Your escrow officer then prepares the documents for you and the seller to sign. New laws in effect require that you, the Buyer, receive the Closing Document (CD) three days before the closing date, for review. If anything in the document changes, closing must be postponed. In this document, you will be told exactly how much money you will need to bring in on the loan. Your Earnest Money will be credited to those costs. You will also be required to provide any **additional documentation the lender needs.**

Oh, and by the way, your employment will be verified, your credit will be pulled once again to see if you have opened new credit and if your credit profile has changed.

Remember that when you apply for the loan, a financial snapshot is made of you. It is ever-changing. The loan is made based on this picture. Do not change it in any way before closing. Read the "10 Do's and Don'ts" daily to stay on course.

Once both you and the sellers have signed the loan documents, they are returned to the lender who reviews them. If everything is satisfactory, the lender funds the loan. The title company records the note and deed of trust and escrow is closed. You should check with country records within a month of closing to make sure that the previous mortgage holder (bank) has been removed. Many times banks are negligent in doing this. It does not mean you assume that loan, however, when you decide to sell the house it will need to be done and causes delays in closing at that time. Avoid any future hassles!

Six Common Ways to Hold Title

Even though only one of you works and are therefore on the loan, Title to the Deed (Property) can be held in both your names. In fact, there are several ways to hold title to the property. In the olden days women could not hold property. If you were an unmarried woman, well, that was even more out of the question. Times have changed.

A Single Man/Woman

A man or woman who are not legally married (i.e. John Doe, a Single Man).

An Unmarried Man/Woman

A man or woman, who having been married, are legally divorced (i.e. John Doe, am Unmarried Man).

A Married Man/Woman, as His/Her Sole and Separate Property

When a married man or woman wishers to acquire title in his or her name alone, the spouse must consent, y quitclaim deed or otherwise, to transfer, thereby relinquishing all right, title and interest in the property (i.e. John Doe, a Married man as his sole and separate property).

Community Property

The Civil Code defines community property as property acquired by husband and wife or either, during marriage when not acquired as the separate property of either. Real property conveyed to a married man o woman is presumed to be community property unless otherwise stated.

Under community property, both spouses have the right by will to dispose of one-half of the community property but all of it will go to the surviving spouse without administration if the other spouse dies without a will. If a spouse exercises his/her right to dispose of one-half, that half is subject to administrations in the estate (i.e. John Doe and Jane Doe, Husband and Wife, as community property).

Joint Tenancy

A joint tenancy estate is defined in the Civil Code as follows. A joint interest is one owned by two or more persons in equal shares by a title created by a single will or transfer, when expressly declared in the will or transfer to be a joint tenancy. A chief characteristic of joint tenancy property immediately vests in the survivor or surviving joint tenants. As a consequence, joint tenancy property is not subject to disposition by will (i.e. John Doe and Jane Doe, Husband and Wife, as Joint Tenants).

Tenancy in Common

Under tenancy in common, the co-owners own individual interest, but unlike joint tenancy, these interests need not be equal in quantity or duration, and may arise from different times. There is no right of survivorship; each tenant owns an interest, which on his or her death vests in his or her heirs or devisees (i.e. John Doe, a Single Man, as to an undivided 3/4ths interest, and George Smith, a Single Man, as to an undivided 1/4th (interest as Tenants in Common)

Conclusion

I hope you have found this book valuable in preparing for home ownership. I have worked as a financial advisor, realtor, and mortgage loan officer with great success. I tell my clients that finding the home is the honeymoon. The hard work comes once your offer is accepted.

Take my advice and start now to evaluate your credit score, accumulate assets for closing costs and reserves, and a down payment if that is part of your strategy. Put yourself in a place of strength to get your offer accepted and to negotiate. If you are not desperate you operate from a place of strength. If you cannot have the home on reasonable terms agreed on by all parties, be prepared to move on to find the next perfect property for you and your family.

As a loan officer, I experienced reluctance and resistance from borrowers getting the documents required to process the loan. It is a painful experience, tedious at best. Start collecting and organizing your documents to alleviate some of the stress. Remember that you are borrowing a great deal of money. This money puts you into a home of your own. Keep the end in mind. And if there are any skeletons in your closet, discuss this with your real estate agent and/or your loan officer. Anything that is there will be sure to come up.

Give all parties the respect and cooperation they need to get you the best outcome possible. You will all be friends in the end. Happy House Buying!

Property Showing Guide

Property Address:	Likes:	Dislikes:
Property Address:	Likes:	Dislikes:
Property Address:	Likes:	Dislikes:
Property Address:	Likes:	Dislikes:
Property Address:	Likes:	Dislikes:
Property Address:	Likes:	Dislikes:
Property Address:	Likes:	Dislikes:
Property Address:	Likes:	Dislikes:

About the Author

 With extensive experience in financial services, real estate and mortgage lending the author uses her expertise to benefit her clients in getting the best deal with the smoothest and most beneficial transaction possible.

Originally from Birmingham, Alabama, Ms. von Klitzing started her career as a Financial Advisor with a Wall Street investment firm. She moved to Germany to complete her doctorate and worked in Europe for 17 years based in Bonn, Stuttgart and Vienna. As President of an international investment company, she expanded markets with a team of 15 serving the needs of US Military, Embassy and United Nations Diplomats, the expatriate community and a broad international clientele throughout Europe, Eastern Europe, the Middle East, Africa and Asia.

In 1996 she moved to New York City and practiced from Wall Street until 2003 when she moved to Florida to take advantage of the real estate boom and become a President's Circle producer, ranking in the top 100 in the nation.

In Atlanta, she specializes mortgage origination and nurtures her fluency in German and French within the international business and social circles. Her international experience is applied to a professional advantage in Georgia's growing prominence as an international center of business and trade.